The Book of Reminders

The Book of Reminders

ANDREW JOHNSTON

Big Day Press

The Book of Reminders. Copyright ©2020 by Andrew Johnston. All rights reserved. Printed in the United States of America.

Quote from Job chapter 42, Christian Standard Bible translation.

Big Day Press
www.bigdaypress.net

For the love that continues to shine on me through my wife and my children, and absolutely refuses to abandon me.

There is that in me--I do not know what it
    is--but I know it is in me.
...
I do not know it--it is without name--it is
    word unsaid,
It is not in any dictionary or utterance or
    symbol.
Walt Whitman

Then Job replied to the Lord:
I know that you can do anything
and no plan of yours can be thwarted.
...
I had heard reports about you,
but now my eyes have seen you.
Therefore, I reject my words and am
    sorry for them;
I am dust and ashes.
The Book of Job

Truth is stranger than fiction, but it is
    because Fiction is obliged to stick to
    possibilities; Truth isn't.
Mark Twain

Introduction

This is not the book I intended to write.

For over two decades, I'd felt a passionate interest in both psychology and religion. I would read book after book, study after study, always searching for one more piece in the big puzzle. Devouring one "explanation book" after another, racing toward a solution that both made sense theoretically and practically worked in the real world. I was searching for the Holy Grail; a "Grand Unified Theory" that would unite religion, psychology, sociology, and my life. Any writing that did not further me in that quest was immediately discarded.

Looking back, it felt very similar to one of the puzzle-style video games I played as a youth. What is the answer to the big question? Where is the ultimate blueprint? What will make sense of all these different areas of life? I was after the double prize of both solving the ultimate puzzle, and practically knowing how to more successfully navigate my personal life.

Since most of my reading has been solutions and formulas and theories, it would be natural to expect my own writing to follow in those same footsteps. What a surprise when it came out sounding like a mix between mystic devotional, repetitive poetry, and wisdom literature!

I guess one could see this book as the brackish water between the rushing river of a relentless "seeker" and the inevitable truth of the eternal ocean. In that place, there is no more destination, no more journey, and no more story. Even as I tell it here in the introduction, the story of this book has a false ring to it. I find myself telling it in the same way I tell "fish stories" to my kids for fun.

The first few passages began as simply notes to myself, helping to maintain a focus on God through my busy and contentious days at work. They were just personal reminders until the words started accumulating. I gave up trying to control the writing process, and eventually there was a distinct sense that it was time to put these reminders in print and join the bigger conversation.

This is no systematic theology or philosophical system, so if you read it looking for internal consistency I'm afraid you'll be disappointed.

I recommend reading this book like you would approach a lunch buffet. Take what you like, leave the rest. Some of it might not agree with you. Some of it might look under cooked. Some of it might cause an allergic reaction. But if you find anything nourishing, and maybe even something refreshing and tasty, then enjoy. Feel free to go back for seconds.

A J
January 2020

Everything is God

Whatever you are looking at right now
    is God

Whatever you are hearing is God
The thought you're having is God
Your fear is God
Your body is God
Your disease is God
Your delight is God
Your worry is God
Your questioning is God
Your family is God
Your friend is God
Your enemy is God

Even your belief in yourself -
    that's God.
And God is complete oneness.

How could you possibly be lost?

The Blessing

The blessing is right in front of you.

It's not resting on a distant mountain top.
It's not buried deep in a priest's robe.
It's not waiting for you in the pages of a
    book.
It's not emanating from a guru's
    forehead.

Everything, in every moment,
    is pulsating with the blessing.
The most sacred text is no more or less
    sacred than your house cat.

Whether you notice or whether you dash
    on with ten things on your mind,
The blessing is complete
    and includes you -
However you are.

Why worry about how to *get* that?

Consistency

Do not confuse consistency
    with authenticity.

I have an alarm system inside,
And when I feel distressed,
It calms down when my thoughts, my
    feelings, and my environment is
    predictable.

Somewhere I learned that others have
    the same alarm system.
They calm down when *I* am predictable!
I learned to be consistent so I wouldn't be
    alone.

But as we grow, we deepen, and we
    change,
And growth is the movement of the
    universe;
Not always comfortable, but something in
    us responds with delight.
Being authentic means having the
    courage to be deeply honest as we
    mature and learn.

Consistency is comfortable.
Authenticity is inspiring.

You Have Nothing To Lose

It can feel like everything is falling apart!
The well-meaning therapist consoles by
    saying, "No, it isn't."
But in fact, it is.

Whatever is currently a "thing"
    is also becoming "not-a-thing"
    or at least a different thing.
Decay, entropy, and dissolution
    are exactly half of the universal
    rhythm.
After birth, death.
After organization, disorganization.
After expansion, contraction.
After growth, decay.

If something has already been created,
    then it is in the process of being
    un-created.
If you believe that you have something
    called "a life,"
    then by definition,
    it is falling apart.

This makes me distressed, but why?

I look back and see how each identity
   must fall apart
   to make way for the next.
The infant fell apart to make way for the
   child,
The child fell apart for the adolescent,
The adolescent for the young adult,
And so on.

Why so distressing as my life falls apart
   yet again?

Here's the distress:
I have a belief that it is *my* life falling
   apart.
In fact, it feels like *I* am falling apart!

All those pieces that define me:
My reputation, possessions,
   relationships, competence, body,
As they fall apart, so will I!

What if **you** are not a thing at all,
   but a process?
Then there is nothing to lose.
Like a river that meets the ocean,
The bounded becomes boundless.
Nothing is lost.

Complete

God is utterly complete.
If God needed anything,
Then there would be something outside
    of God,
Which is impossible for the One True
    God.

God is fully everywhere.
If God was approachable,
    or in any way distant,
    or more in one place and less in
    another,
Then that would mean God is something
    that fits into space,
(meaning space is somehow bigger than
    God)
Which is impossible for the One True
    God.

God is creating everything.
If a single thought in your head did not
    come directly from God,
Then there would be a creative power
    that is not God,
Which is impossible for the One True
    God.

All Opinions Are Relative

God is unconditional and universal love.
    Fully complete.
In full completeness, there is no space for
    distinctions.
Without distinctions, there is no division.
Without division, there can be no
    preference.
Without preference, no opinion.

Thus, in God's ultimate completeness,
    there can be no opinions.

When we talk of God's preferences or
    God's desires,
We are not *wrong,*
We are simply talking on another level.

For of course there are energies of good
    and evil.
There is health and decay.
There is violence and harmony.
There is love and hate.

And at that level of good and evil,
There may indeed be a one-sided god of
    good,
Who watches over us
    and longs for things like redemption
    and praise and justice.

But let's be clear:
The ultimate God, who is all in all,
Who is fully complete,
Contains everything, and *is* everything.

Where, in completeness, is there any
    room for an opinion?

Any opinion, judgment, or preference
    emerges from a limited being,
And not from the One True God.

Thus, your sins are forgiven.
Because in God's eyes,
They never existed.

It's All Energy

Mass = Energy divided by the speed of
    light squared

Your solid body isn't really.
Minuscule pockets of energy
    bound together by more energy.

More similar to a flowing river than to
    solid ground.
Each shift causing ripples that impact
    everything else.

It's all connected -
    your thoughts and memories
    the other person in the room
    the breakfast you ate
    (and all the plants and animals your
        breakfast came from)
    the war in Syria
    the love for your kids
    the moon's orbit...

Your not-solid body of energy bundles
    is flowing among the ocean of energy
Can you feel the moving tides as they
    carry your body,
And play upon your mind?

The Rule of Distress

Fear of public speaking,
Workaholism,
Arrogant self-promotion,
Codependent behaviors,
Needing to always be in control,
Fear of missing out,
Angry jealousy,
Substance abuse...

All branches of the same tree.
If you can recognize this,
> psychopathology suddenly becomes very simple.

The human nervous system is built to set off distress when it feels threatened,
And to eliminate that distress as soon as possible.

There are five categories of threats:
Anatomical (the physical body),
Attachment (close relationships),
Agency (control of the immediate environment),
Affiliation (connection to a community),
Achievement (able to provide and be respected).

A person caught in "control mode" can be infuriating.
Someone ruled by their anxiety can make you frustrated.
Enmeshed, dependent spouses can be challenging.

However, none of this is their fault.
They are just responding to the human nervous system's fundamental rule of distress:
You *must* reduce the body distress level, by any means necessary.

Cave Paintings

Don't confuse God with that which is not
    yet understood.

The ancients worshiped the "holy men"
who could draw images of bison
    on rock walls.
Now, even a three-year-old can do that.

Effective energy workers, gurus, and faith
    healers
Are simply practicing a type of medicine
    that will be common-place for the
    generations to come.

Think about it:
Some "enlightened beings" can still give
    you bad advice
And misdirect you when giving directions
    to the train station.
Someone who is "full of the Spirit" can
    still have the personality of a
    complete ass,
And can assault a subordinate.

Heed the wisdom of the early Christian
    monastic who said,
"Seek God, and not where God lives."
Don't confuse these "special" abilities
    with holiness!

If you get distracted by astonishing deeds
    or powerful words,
You will miss the God who is equally
    everywhere and always.

Even in you. Completely.

Fairness

"It isn't fair!"
I've said it out loud, and silently inside.
I've said it about myself, and about others.
I've said it when things are good, and when things are bad.

What is this notion of fairness?
My dog knows nothing of it.
The bird at the feeder knows nothing of it.
No plant or animal knows anything about "fairness,"
Because it only exists in the human mind.

Just like "rights" and "justice" and "deserving"
Fairness is simply a verbal tool -
Leverage in a debate when trying to convince someone to change their behavior.
It isn't real!

When my little sister's ice cream bowl was bigger,
My imagination created a dream
Desire replaced gratitude

I thought, "I want more!"
But I learned it's more effective to say
    "It's not fair."

When I first saw someone who lives on
    the street, homeless,
My empathy created a dream
I thought, "I want to see her happy."
And I learned it's more effective to say
    "It's not fair."

Then, sometimes, a toxic thought appears
    in the mind,
one that can haunt people for their entire
    lives,
Stealing their energy, crushing their
    gratitude, and causing unnecessary
    pain:

Things should be fair!

Free yourself from this thought, and live
    with more power and grace.
Release this thought, and escape the
    useless preoccupation it causes.
Use it as an effective verbal tool if you
    like,
But the universe neither knows nor cares
    a thing about fairness.

The Fear of Missing Out

The chicken panics to return to her flock.
The young gazelle, briefly distracted,
    sprints full speed to rejoin the herd.
The ground squirrel chirps in distress
    when he discovers he's alone.

Me too.

I feel safer when included.
If my schedule makes me stressed and
    miserable,
At least I'm not missing out.

The lemming says,
Even if we're running off a cliff,
    at least I'm not running alone!

Fear is Nothing to Fear

Your fear is just fear.
Your shame is just shame.
Your hurt is just hurt.
Your hopelessness is just hopelessness.
Your despair is just despair.

No need to add meaning,
    and make more of it than it is.

The deep despair felt by your ancestors,
    where is it today?
Where is their fear, shame and hurt?
Gone. Just like yours will be.

The impacts of their despair can be seen,
but the feelings have vanished like
    smoke,
And don't mean anything at all.

If despair is with you, no need to deny it.
(Denying any feeling corrupts and
    magnifies it, of course.)
Let it be there.

Just no need to make more of it than it is.

The Myth of Me

You are not in danger,
Because there is no **_you_**.

Being rejected and shamed,
Looking weak, helpless and stupid,
Getting attacked in the street,
Contracting a life-threatening disease...

I'm not saying to stop taking precautions.
Don't be naive.

What I am saying is this:
The **_you_** who remains preoccupied with
  your individual safety, success, and
  survival,
Only appears to be something.
It doesn't actually exist.

A body exists, which is distinct from
  other bodies,
With distinctive patterns of thought and
  physical form.
But the **_you_** who feels worried about
  yourself
Is a mental feedback loop;
An assumption based on a pattern of
  thought.

Simply a by-product of the brain's ability to self-reflect.

It's closer to true to say that the feeling of a separate *you* is actually a process,
Like a running software program.
It's not a thing that exists on its own.

(Of course, this worried, self-concerned process of *you* is also part of the perfection of God!)
But so is the inevitable questioning of it.

If the bodymind is truly at risk,
Then it employs fear and anger to stay safe and alive -
Valuable resources for survival!

It's only in the feedback loop of the imagined *you*
Where fear becomes anxiety and anger becomes bitterness or rage.

Imaginary threats setting off responses from an imaginary self.

Freedom

Any freedom that can be achieved
    is not the ultimate freedom.
Any freedom that can be pursued
    is not the ultimate freedom.

The ultimate freedom is already here.

Freedom isn't yours, because the ultimate
    freedom is this:
There is no separate ***you***
    so who can be not-free?

Of course, we work for all the freedoms:
    political, financial, relational,
    religious.
Equality, liberation and justice,
    what powerful expressions of love!
Don't cop out on your chance to
    cooperate in these expressions of
    love.

Since the ultimate freedom is already
    here,
You are free to give yourself to this work.

The father hears his child calling for him,
 but is so busy fighting to free himself
 that he cannot respond!
Only when he wakes up in his bed, and
 realizes that his bondage was part of
 the dream, can he go to his child.

Focus on being stuck, and you focus on
 the dream.
Focus on yourself, and you focus on the
 dream.
Listen instead for the call of your child.
Listen instead for the freedom beyond
 you.

You Don't Need to Think About Yourself

It's been said that teaching a pig to sing
>is both a waste of time

And an annoyance to the pig.

Concerned thinking about yourself works
>the same way.

It is generally pointless
>and gets you all worked up over a
>*you* that doesn't really exist at all.

Utter futility.

This Incident, Too, Is God

You don't have to give anything to God.
You don't have to manage your thoughts.
You don't have to appear competent,
    friendly, successful, or relaxed.
You don't have to worry.
You don't have to *stop* worrying.

You don't even have to be yourself.

You get to simply be.
Because every single thing in this
    moment is God.
The other people, the noises you hear, the
    events unfolding, the next words to
    be said, the sensation in your gut,
    every thought and comparison and
    worry in your head,
ALL of it is God.

And God is thoroughly unconcerned.
God simply is all of it!
God simply *is.*

It's Not as Complex as You Think

"All thoughts have the same root.
Find that one and you can defeat all the rest."

All your frustration,
Which leads to all your theories,
Which leads to all your plans,
Which builds more history,
And makes more frustration,
Is all emerging from a single thought.

Instead of struggling with my history, my thought patterns, my feelings, my reputation, my frustration, my desires,
What if "my" was gone?

Then all the history, patterns, feelings, and the rest
Become forces of nature,
Blowing through your mind like dry leaves in a gust of wind.

Turning to Face It

What would happen if,
The next time you found yourself in an
    awkward social situation,
Stomach dropping,
Heart racing,
They all give you *that look*...

What if,
Instead of doing the usual thing you do
    trying to relieve the tension
(talking, leaving, distracting, explaining)
What if you simply name the discomfort
    underneath it all,
Recognize your freedom,
And say to yourself:

"This, too, is God."

The Labeling Game

The mind loves convenience
    and it loves distinctions
    and it loves safety.
It can find all three in the labeling game.

Preachers and politicians are the masters
    of this game.
It's easy to play:
Claim the authority to label someone by
    doing so,
And by labeling someone as "them" you
    create a sense of unity between "us".

This type of authority is cheap, of course
This type of unity is fragile and
    temporary.
These game-players do create a sense of
    safety for their followers,
And will likely grow in worldly power,
But for the one who has seen the truth,
    the game is over.

Labels come flying at you, like angry
    crows looking for a perch,
But they no longer find anywhere to land.
They fly on, squawking into the distance.

Timing

Was the Earth created billions of years
 ago?
Or six thousand years ago?

Neither! It is being created right now.

Creation never happened,
Because the past only exists as a thought,
A thought which is being created right
 now.

It is your mind experiencing something
 that it calls Earth,
And it is your mind experiencing
 sensations that it calls Me.
Without your mind's activity of naming
 these experiences,
There would be only God, the E-ternal,
 outside of time.

The Eternal God has no age.
Only this, only now.

Words

The true nature of reality is undivided.
Yet words, by their nature, divide.

A word means "this"
    and therefore implies "not that".
"Running" means not walking or sitting.
"Thinking" means not "not thinking".
"Cat" means one specific organism,
    not the couch he's on,
    nor the meal he ate earlier,
    nor the dirt his body will become.

Words are dividing tools,
    like cookie-cutters for experience.
Essential for day-to-day tasks
    like baking cookies!

But that's why words will never, ever, be
    able to fully communicate the true
    nature of reality.
They can only hint and point.

No cookie-cutter, however big, can
    possibly encompass everything.
We're living inside the ultimate cookie!
Where our words fail, and we go silent,
God is.

Jesus

When someone uses the name "Jesus"
 you don't really know what exactly
 they are referring to.
Is it an inner voice of intuition and
 guidance?
Is it the historical man from Palestine?
Is it a collection of religious expectations
 embodied?
Is it a promise of future justice after
 being treated unjustly?
Is it a super-powered mascot, inwardly
 reassuring that they have chosen the
 winning team?
Is it a fairy tale figure that they have now
 outgrown?
Is it a point of reference for the eternal,
 pulling them out of their trivial daily
 stressors?

Don't just assume you know what they
 mean!
The word itself is merely a label.
When you begin to listen for the
 meanings behind the word,
Then your conversations will reflect the
 compassion and clarity attributed to
 Jesus.

Death

The human system is built to survive,
Just like other animals.
So of course the mind reacts to a threat
    by strengthening the body to run.
We call it "fear"

The human system also has the unique
    capacity to imagine -
It can imagine something called "the
    future".
And it can imagine something called
    "death"

From this mix of animal and human, we
    get the special ability to be
    preoccupied with the fear of death.

But the future is just imagined!
It doesn't exist.
And death is also imagined!
It's just a name for a change in patterns -
    when one process ends
    and others begin.

No future. No death.
Nothing to lose,
No death to fear.

Treating Others as Yourself

Infants learn to recognize "me"
Children learn to recognize "you"
Adolescents learn to recognize "us" and
 "them"
Adults can come to recognize the whole,
Which obliterates any distinction
 between "me" and "you".

Of what use are ethical rules for one who
 sees this truth?
"You" are God
"I" am God
There is nothing at all but God!

No need to try loving others
 as you would love yourself.
God becomes all,
 and Love simply is.

Love simply is.

Prayer

Any god who can be pleased by your
    prayers
Is not the One True God.
Likewise for any god who can be
    disappointed by your lack of prayer.

There may be an entity that exists
    beyond our awareness
Who delights in us, wants the best for us,
    protects us from evil, and desires
    praise.
There might be many! Who knows?

We cannot know them any better than a
    tomato plant knows the gardener.
It simply tastes the fertilized soil,
    feels the pruning shears,
    bears fruit in season.

But do not confuse these gardeners with
    the One True God -
Unconditional love,
    without name or form.
Because the One True God
    is ALL names and ALL forms.
All in all.

The Pointless Gospel

The only message that truly deserves to
    be called "Good News" is this:
God is all.

If God is all,
    nothing can be incomplete.
If God is all,
    there is nothing anyone needs to
    achieve.
If God is all,
    there is no separate *me* who could
    achieve anything in the first place!

Nothing incomplete,
Nothing to achieve,
No *me*

The Good News affirms that since God is
    ALL, there is nothing you need in
    order to be spiritually complete,
Including hearing the Good News!

The true Gospel is therefore
    utterly, wonderfully pointless.

Leverage

Blame, victimhood, domination, shaming,
    inferiority, intellectual debate,
    labeling, citing scripture, violence,
    political influence, bribery,
    marginalizing, ignoring, threatening...

All simply the attempt to get what I need,
    when I don't trust that simply asking
    will be successful.

The infant asks with complete
    vulnerability.
Adults have learned the danger of being
    vulnerable:
We use leverage instead!

If you want to find greater intimacy,
    and stop offending people,
Take lessons from an infant.

Impossible Tasks

You can't be "in the present"
    any more than you can "let go"

Past and future are simply memories and
    imagination.
There is nothing but this!
Time is a story that we construct in our
    minds.
So where is a time called "the present"
    for you to be in?

Physical objects like wealth and goods,
    and mental objects like memories
    and desires,
Are only made of energy -
    energy that constantly changes like
    the swirling ripples of a river.
So what is there to let go of?

Relieved from impossible tasks,
Reality just is.

Freedom!

Shame

A structural engineer understands failure
    as the logical result of an equation.
A scientist understands failure as one
    possible outcome of a successful
    experiment.
A salesperson understands failure as a
    required element on their way to
    achieving success.

Why then, does the fear of failure hold us
    hostage?
Because it hurts, of course!

I want to succeed and realize my desires.
And I want to know myself as a success.
And I want to be known by others as a
    success.

When I reach for a desire and I fail,
    my mind responds to the hurt by
    doing its job: explaining.
Then when the explanation is that "I am a
    failure," we call it shame.

And since the mind wants to prove itself
    right, shame becomes toxic.

Friends try reassuring you that you are
> not a failure.
Therapists help you discover where the
> shame originated.
Preachers tell you that God loves you
> regardless.

In contrast, this message here is
> ultimately liberating,
And also completely hopeless.

You don't exist,
> so how could you be a failure?
You can't be a failure,
> any more than you can be a success.
You aren't anything but a thought
> emerging from the mind of God.

Watch the labels drift away
> like wakes on the sea.

Spiritual Advice

In order to properly diagram a sentence,
    you need instruction.
To rebuild an engine, you need a teacher.
To become more mindful,
    you need to practice.
To lead a religious community,
    you need a mentor with
    organizational skills.

To meet the One True God,
    advice doesn't help,
    teaching misdirects,
    practice is a waste of time.

The One True God cannot be approached
    because the One True God is
    everything!
Your longing to approach God
    is already God!

Spiritual advice merely plays into the
    myth that God is somewhere else
    and can be approached.
Absurd.

Living unadvised, the Spirit of God winks
    at you from everywhere.

No Right or Wrong Way to Worship

Religion is:
A collection of stories
A safe haven of the like-minded
A result of eating the fruit of "the Knowledge of Good and Evil"
A structure in which to mature; a series of cocoons to outgrow
A safety net
An ongoing conversation
An excuse to kill
A game of boundaries
A set of practices and tools for maintaining psychological health
A repository of useless opinions
A language for what's impossible to put into words
A place where human flowering and human decay exist simultaneously
A place to share in the delight of community
A purely human activity, by humans, for humans, and completely irrelevant to the One True God.

The Story

Have you noticed the distress that hides
    in your story?

Sometimes, you actually are being
    attacked, and your body puts you into
    distress to escape or fight!
The rest of the time, it's just a reaction to
    the story in your mind.

What is the past? Just a mix of memory
    and meaning.
The future? Imagination.
With no past or future, there's no story!

Actors are free to live fully into their roles
Because they know that the story only
    exists in the play.
When they step off the stage,
    they leave behind all the distress that
    had occupied them so completely.

The actor drops a copy of the screenplay
    onto the stage and walks toward the
    exit.

Such is the fate of all my opinions,
     injuries, and worries -
Destined to be shed, dropped, and
     forgotten.

Only God remains.

Implications

If God is truly everywhere, everything, always,
Then what does that *mean?*
What should we do differently?

Should we stop trying to reach God?
Should we stop evangelizing?
Should we stop longing for change?
Should we stop working for justice?
Should we stop listening to advice?
Should we stop trying to improve ourselves?
Should we stop having preferences?

No! No shoulds at all.
It simply means that this is all God.
God is everywhere, everything, always.
Even your attempt to find meanings and implications.

For if the One True God is truly God, then that includes you.
All your opinions, habits, desires, relationships, memories, hopes, and patterns you call "my life" -
That's God too.
No need to find implications.

Impulse, Calculation, and Intuition

How do you know when you're hungry?

There is a knowing that supersedes our
    calculations.
There is a drive toward what is healthy
    and away from the unhealthy.
Our calculating mind cannot fully
    understand it.
This is the knowing in the body.

The primitive limbic brain is impulsive -
    it responds quickly to relieve distress.
It will reach for a healthy relief,
    like a trusted friend,
Or an unhealthy relief,
    like an addictive substance.
It doesn't care which one -
    it's only job is to relieve the distress.

The human cortex is calculating -
    it can respond with more
    understanding.
It can interpret the context, consider
    history, think about future impacts.
But it also creates meaning
    which can be helpful or damaging.

The body as a whole includes not only
> the brain, but also the organs, cells,
> fluids, patterns, and any energy
> systems that we have yet to name.
The body can respond with intuition
> which is a more integrated knowing.

Neither the limbic brain nor the cortex
> can grasp the full-body intuition.
The cortex can't explain it, and it typically
> ignores what it can't explain.
The limbic brain, when distressed,
> ignores anything that it doesn't see as
> bringing immediate relief.

So intuition stands as the best and most
> difficult guidance to hear.
The still, small voice.

Spiritual Practice

The One True God is everywhere,
> everything, always.

Nothing can possibly bring you any closer
> to God than you are now.

Then is there any point to spiritual
> practice? Of course!

The point of spiritual practice could be:
To feel part of a tradition.
To have a conversation starter.
To become less impulsive.
To develop valuable personal traits, like
> empathy, forbearance, wisdom.

To create a bond with other practitioners.
To earn credibility and a sense of
> accomplishment.

To generate mystical experiences.

Each tradition is a full toolbox,
> a playground of options for you.

All existing within the never-ending
> expanse of unconditional love,

Which remains exactly the same before,
> during, and after your spiritual
> practice.

Teaching

The highest truth cannot be taught.
In fact, teachings are an excellent method
    for remaining distracted from it!

Any enlightenment that has a method,
    is not the true enlightenment.
Any salvation that has a prerequisite,
    is not the true salvation.
Any teacher who believes themselves to
    be closer to God than you,
    is just playing ego games.

Feel free to delight in new teaching!
Grow in maturity and develop skill.
One of the most enjoyable elements of
    this life is to evolve!
Learn to dance, learn to meditate,
Learn to love well, learn to play,
Learn to cook, learn to write,
Learn to give, learn to speak.

You'll never learn the highest truth.

Trying to learn the highest truth is like
    asking people in Times Square to
    show you the way to New York.
The very premise is absurd.

The Helpful Guardian

Your intellect is there for your protection!

It stands at the door with a keen eye and
    hand resting on the sword hilt, asking
    for credentials.
"To get access to my sensitive heart,
    you must first satisfy my guardian."

When it's doing its job, the intellect
    protects you from unsafe lovers, false
    friends, and bad deals.

How vital your intellect is for religion!
Con men, narcissists who disguise their
    ego as God, cult leader wannabes,
    devotees hoping to use your
    conversion to reassure themselves,
    and just the fervent gullible ones.
Your intellect guardian can help you
    avoid trouble from all these.

Be grateful for such a loyal friend!

It has worked so hard
    to understand and predict,
    to improve and control,
    to develop a castle of safety for you.

What a jarring moment, then, as the
  eternal ocean tide comes in,
To learn that its castle fortress was made
  of sand,
To see its magnificent theories rinsed
  away by the waves.

Deep down you know the frightening,
  liberating truth:
You really will be forgotten.
Don't miss out on your opportunity to be
  utterly pointless!

Your intellect may object.
If so, simply thank your loyal guardian,
  and tell her you didn't need that
  castle of safety anyway.
Reassure her that there's no way you can
  be threatened,
Because there is no *you* and never was.

At the core, there's nothing there that can
  be endangered.

Irony

The man who loudly insists that the evil
 deeds of tyrants,
And the arrogant selfishness of the
 wealthy,
And the dangerous words of heretics,
And the unfair violence of extremists,
Absolutely, positively CANNOT be God,

is also God.

Free Will

Look inside and you'll find a long board balanced like a see-saw above the water.
On one end, a beautiful self-absorbed prince,
On the other end, a miserable leper.

The prince is your pride.
He takes credit for your success and feels proud and important.
The leper is your shame, who takes blame for your failings and feels worthless and stupid.

Too much prince, and you're arrogant.
Too much leper, and you beat yourself up.
How do you maintain a healthy balance?

Ha! Trick question.

The board they both stand upon is free will.
The fulcrum under the board is the belief in *me*.

Remove the fulcrum, and watch them all
  drop into the water.
Pride falls in.
Shame falls in.
The belief in free will falls in.
Nothing left but ripples in the water.

Without *me* to hinge upon,
  they all disappear.

Then who is left to need a healthy
  balance?

What Shall I Do, Then?

The mind reflexively reaches for the
    question in moments of distress.
Like the protective impulse of a mother
    reaching for her crying baby.
Like the time-worn habit of the soldier
    sighting his gun.
Like the ritual of the recovering alcoholic,
    lighting a cigarette.

"So what shall I do?" the mind asks.

An impulse to soothe the pain of the
    moment.
An impulse to protect ones self from
    pointless academic theories that have
    no practical application.
An impulse to live better by doing the
    right thing.

"What shall I do?"

God is the only one who does anything.
If you want to know what God will do,
    just stop asking and watch.

The Richness Simply Is

A moment during worship when my
    mind notices a shift happening inside.
This place, this music, these people.
Time begins to slow down.
An opening sensation in the torso.
Old feelings and memories emerge and
    intertwine with the present.
Nostalgia and eternity,
Deepening,
Integration.

The mind recognizes what has happened.
This place has become *home.*
Tears well up as the recognition deepens
    the experience.

Such richness!

But not a richness *for me*.

Simply richness. Simply peacefulness.
Simply delight. Simply gratitude.

Joy untarnished by thoughts of *me*.

Irrelevant Shame

Babies are not born with a
 self-destructive shame voice.
So where did mine come from?

A distant parent?
A traumatic moment on the school bus?
A forgotten abuse?
A corrupted instinct to be socially
 acceptable?
An agent of spiritual warfare?
A chemical imbalance?

Turns out, it doesn't matter.
Just a fictitious thought pattern accusing
 a fictitious me, based on a past that
 doesn't exist!

With no target left to accuse, and no past
 evidence to bring,
It gradually fades,
Like a prosecutor who slowly recognizes
 she is speaking to an empty
 courtroom.

Judgment

I notice my thoughts of scorn as another
    driver rips past and cuts me off.
Likewise for world leaders, business
    executives, and political
    commentators.

They enrage me!
A mix of righteous anger, personal
    offense, and a big assumption:
"They should know better!"

Feel the anger? Fine!
    Sometimes people need to be
    confronted.
Feel offended? Sure!
    Acknowledge the hurt of being
    ignored and walked on.
It will help you identify with the
    oppressed if you can really feel that
    pain.

But what about the assumption that they
    should know better?
"Should" says more about me than about
    them.

It's a symptom of judgment,
> which is the auto-immune disease of the soul.

Judgment falls apart when recognizing the truth -
That other person is a manifestation of the complete and perfect God.

Race on by, inconsiderate driver.
My protective anger keeps my family safe as I avoid the danger.
My offended ego reminds me of how painful it is to be ignored.

But the old assumption:
"She should know better!"
It sounds absurd now, even comical!
Like blaming my sunburn on Apollo's vindictive wrath.

"Should" is based on the illusion of choice.
It is worse than useless.

Scripture

There is no meaning in scripture.
Meaning only happens in the mind of the reader!

The mind searches and connects,
 making intellectual meaning from the words.
The body reacts with emotion:
 tears, excitement, anger, joy - these create a more powerful meaning.
The book itself, however, simply lies flat on the table.
It has no more meaning hidden among the pages than an appliance manual.

The one who sees this truth
 has shifted her reverence from the lifeless words,
And begins to honor the alchemy of word, memory, community, and connection happening inside the reader.

Words only earn the title of scripture
 when that internal response makes them so.

Invitation

These words get you nowhere.
Don't expect them to change you.

When this is recognized, the bodymind
    relaxes.
There's nowhere to get to;
    you're already in God.
There's no ***you*** to change;
    just patterns of thought and biology.

These words are simply an invitation to
    celebrate our freedom.

The Image of God

You weren't actually created in the image of God.
There wasn't a time where God looked in a heavenly mirror, reached into the clay, and fashioned a human body to that resemblance.

There is no space between Creator and created!
There is no past time when creation happened!

You are not created in the image of God.
God simply is.
No image.
No creating.
No you.

God simply is.

Believing in History

Jonah was called to Assyria
    because it was their time to change.
The voice of truth told him so,
    the truth of the situation.
But Jonah had another voice,
    the voice of history,
Saying, "They will probably kill you."
And one more voice,
    the voice of his woundedness,
Saying, "They abused you, they don't
    deserve forgiveness!"

What an interesting trio, these three:
    truth, history, and woundedness.
I have them too, of course.

Woundedness, flouting his bandages like
    a purple heart,
Trying amid his pain to care for me
    (which always looks like resentment
    and distance to others)

History, with his perfect recall of every
    time I've felt overwhelmed by
    loneliness, poverty, and shame.
Trying desperately to keep me safe and
    prepared for the worst

(which always looks like anxiety and
suspicion to others)

And truth, wide-eyed and soft-spoken,
Unfazed by how anything "should" be.
At times wary, or loving, or grieving, or
excited.
Always completely free and honest,
but not always heard.
(Sometimes I wish for Jonah's giant fish
forcing me to stop and listen)

Now, the easy moral to this fable is that
we should all listen to the voice of
truth, because that is really the voice
of God.
That moral fits with my Sunday School
curriculum, and gives me a goal to
work toward.

However, if we're talking about the One
True God,
Then ALL of my voices are the voice of
God.
Surrounded on all sides by utter holiness!
Even within!
Drowning in completeness, what goal
could I possibly find to work for?
The Divine fish has had me all along.

Getting In Touch With Yourself

There is an experience common to all humans.
It's referred to by different names:
wholeness, grounding, authenticity, core state, mindfulness.

It is found by essentially defying your natural defenses.
Instead of the rush of fear,
slow down and listen.
Instead of the dulling of depression,
step boldly into your fears.

The "false self" is built on fear.
That's why accessing the "authentic self" requires facing the fear and stepping through.

But how can I do that?
I can't. God does it.

God is the authentic self.
God is the false self.
God is the fear.
And sometimes, God steps through.

Enjoy the ride.

<u>Love</u>

All this talk about God,
    but what about love?

You don't need to search for love,
    or make love happen,
    or try to love,
    or learn how to love.

How hard does the fish in the ocean have
    to search in order to find water?

Now, romantic love does take effort.
Sentimental love you can learn.
The human love, which means helping
    one another feel safe, accepted and
    adored -
That love can indeed be learned and
    developed as a skill.

But unconditional love, divine love,
    ultimate acceptance -
That love hides right in front of our faces
    with its humble labels:
Energy, Matter, Me, You, Everything.

What could you possibly do to find
    everything?

Apology

If you have looked here for a path to
    salvation or enlightenment,
I apologize.

These words have no more usefulness
    than a warm breeze,
    or a car horn,
    or a runny nose.
Don't expect any deep, hidden meanings.

Words do nothing, because there is only
    one do-er.
These words are just the song of a
    mockingbird in a distant tree.
If you find any of it gratifying,
    delight in the gratification.
If you disagree with any of it,
    delight in the disagreement!

Just remember,
You will never merge with God,
    because there is no separate you.
There is no time in which you can merge.
No me.
No story.

God alone is.

About the author

Andrew Johnston lives with his wife, two children, a dog and a cat in Greenville, SC. He has a theology degree from Emory University and a psychotherapy degree from Eastern Mennonite University, and has worked as a Mennonite pastor, a full-time volunteer with Habitat for Humanity, a software salesperson, and a stay-at-home Dad. He currently works as a therapist at a private practice in downtown Greenville. He is no longer on social media, but you can send him an email at: bookofreminders@gmail.com

www.ingramcontent.com/pod-product-compliance
Lightning Source LLC
Chambersburg PA
CBHW052114070526
44584CB00017B/2478